A MESSAGE TO YOUNG AMERICA'S FOUNDATION SUPPORTERS

Dear Friends,

Thank you for your support of Young America's Foundation and the Reagan Ranch. We hope you enjoy this special photo book by Newt and Callista Gingrich and David Bossie. It is a token of our appreciation for all you do to help us preserve the Reagan Ranch and share President Reagan's ideas and lasting accomplishments with increasing numbers of young Americans.

Speaker Gingrich is a great friend to Young America's Foundation. He regularly addresses our student audiences at the National Conservative Student Conference, CPAC, and on college campuses nationwide. We were honored to host Newt and Callista at the Reagan Ranch as they filmed the award-winning documentary, *Ronald Reagan: Rendezvous with Destiny*. This important film—produced in partnership with Citizens United—documents the life and lasting accomplishments of President Reagan.

This special photo book includes over 140 images from the making of this film, much of which was filmed at Rancho del Cielo.

Lou Cannon said it best: *"There's more of Ronald Reagan in this ranch than in all the speeches he ever gave."*

Your continued support allows us to pass on President Reagan's values and ideas through our work at the Reagan Ranch and nationwide, and we are honored to partner with you in this shared cause.

We hope you enjoy this book, and we thank you, again, for your generous support of Young America's Foundation and the Reagan Ranch.

Sincerely,

Ron Robinson, PRESIDENT
YOUNG AMERICA'S FOUNDATION

RONALD REAGAN
Rendezvous with Destiny

RONALD REAGAN
Rendezvous with Destiny

NEWT GINGRICH

CALLISTA GINGRICH

DAVID N. BOSSIE

Michelle Selesky, Editor
Dain Valverde, Photographic Editor

DUNHAM
books

For information about bulk purchases or licensing of
Ronald Reagan: Rendezvous with Destiny,
please contact the publisher:

DUNHAM BOOKS
63 Music Square East
Nashville, Tennessee 37203
dunhambooks@dunhamgroupinc.com

Edited by Michelle Selesky
Photographic editing by Dain Valverde and Callista Gingrich

Printed in Canada
ISBN 978-1-4507-4672-4

To President and Mrs. Reagan
who dedicated their lives to America
and the cause of freedom.

TABLE OF CONTENTS

Introduction

As America marks the 100th birthday of President Ronald Reagan, we are pleased to bring you this unique photographic collection, inspired by our documentary film, *Ronald Reagan: Rendezvous with Destiny*, to honor the life and legacy of our nation's 40th President.

Over three decades have passed since Ronald Reagan was first elected to the White House, yet the impact of his leadership is still evident today. While in office, President Reagan had three major goals — to restore the economy, to revive the American spirit, and to defeat the Soviet Union. Remaining true to his convictions and believing in the American people, Reagan accomplished these goals.

Yet Ronald's Reagan's legacy encompasses far more than his achievements as President. Throughout the many chapters of his life, all of which played a role in molding his political beliefs, Reagan never failed to display the character, integrity, and optimism that helped him to become one of the greatest leaders in modern history.

As Thomas Evans describes in his book, *The Education of Ronald Reagan*, one of the most influential periods of Ronald Reagan's life came as his acting career was ending and he became a spokesperson for General Electric. This eight-year period with G.E. from 1954 until 1962 had a significant impact on forging Reagan's convictions and conservative beliefs.

Giving hundreds of speeches on free market principles to thousands of workers across the country, Ronald Reagan honed his beliefs in support of free enterprise, at the same time he was leading union workers as the President of the Screen Actors Guild. Reagan, a former FDR Democrat, would become the Republican Governor of California in 1966.

Ten years later, after gaining valuable experience working with a Democratic legislature in

Sacramento, Ronald Reagan sought the Republican nomination for President and narrowly lost to the incumbent, President Gerald Ford. Yet even after defeat, Reagan shared a message of patriotism and hope, "We must go forth from here united, determined that what a great general said a few years ago is true: There is no substitute for victory."

Finally, in 1980, at the age of sixty-nine, Ronald Reagan was elected to the White House, offering a new vision for America based on principled leadership and faith in the American people. In the midst of the Cold War, when the Soviet Union seemed permanent and unchallengeable, Reagan boldly called on President Gorbachev to "tear down this wall," and marked the beginning of the end of the Soviet Union.

Through major challenges and triumphs, Ronald Reagan is remembered for his endless optimism. James A. Baker, Chief of Staff and Treasury Secretary under President Reagan, remembers, "Throughout his presidency, even into the last days of the second term, he always had that wonderful sense of humor and the ability to disarm people."

Even as President Reagan shared his personal battle with Alzheimer's with the nation, he left us with a message of hope. "I now begin the journey that will lead me into the sunset of my life. I know that for America there will always be a bright dawn ahead. Thank you, my friends. May God always bless you."

Thanks to Ronald Reagan, there is indeed a bright dawn ahead for America.

Margaret Thatcher said it best upon President Reagan's passing, "We have one beacon to guide us that Ronald Reagan never had. We have his example."

President Ronald Reagan continues to serve as a shining example of a principled leader who believed deeply in America and the American people. Through this photographic collection, we hope you will find renewed inspiration from a remarkable man who made a profound impact upon our nation and the world.

Ronald Wilson Reagan
Life Before The Presidency

Reagan Family Christmas Card, from left to right: Jack Reagan, Neil Reagan, Ronald Reagan (with "Dutch" haircut), and Nelle Reagan, circa 1916-1917

Ronald Reagan (hand on chin in front row) posing with other family members, 1920s

Ronald Reagan was born in Tampico, Illinois, in an apartment above the local bank on February 6, 1911. The family moved frequently. Reagan later wrote, "I was forever the new kid in school. We moved to wherever my father's ambition took him." They eventually settled in nearby Dixon, Illinois.

Ronald Reagan's hometown, Dixon, Illinois

"I think Reagan's core values came from Dixon. I think they were inside of Reagan. This view of America as this land of opportunity, he carried them through his political incarnations. They were there as a Democrat. They were there as a Republican." LOU CANNON

Ronald Reagan in Dixon, Illinois, 1920s

Reagan's journey from his childhood in Illinois to his career in Hollywood is a purely American story.

Formal photograph of Ronald Reagan, 1934

Ambitious and hardworking, Reagan had enough talent and luck to succeed.

Ronald Reagan stars as 'George Gipp' in *Knute Rockne-All American,* 1940

Reagan's political journey began when the Screen Actors Guild elected him President, recognizing a skilled leader and negotiator. As President of the Screen Actors Guild, Reagan took a strong stand against Communism.

Engagement photograph of Ronald Reagan and Nancy Davis, January 1952

Ronald and Nancy Reagan with Bill and Ardis Holden after the Reagans' wedding at the Holdens' house in Toluca Lake, California, March 4, 1952

Ronald Reagan visits Nancy Reagan on the set of her movie, *Donovan's Brain*, 1953

Ronald Reagan and *General Electric Theater*, 1954-1962

When Reagan's acting career was coming to a close, he gratefully accepted a job as spokesman for General Electric, expertly promoting General Electric's innovations.

"He was a pitchman, so being a pitchman he got pretty good at giving a pitch. And he was always comfortable in front of a camera. And being comfortable in front of a camera is part of the modern presidency, and so he was a natural."

WILLIAM J. BENNETT

Ronald Reagan visits a General Electric plant in Danville, Illinois, October 1955

On the road for General Electric, Reagan met with thousands of hardworking Americans. His speeches, which he wrote himself, focused on the benefits of the free market system. Over the next eight years, Reagan honed his speeches and began to focus on the incompetence of big government. Reagan, a longtime Democrat and admirer of Franklin Delano Roosevelt, found his politics were changing as well.

"He learned from the workers themselves about some of the regulatory problems, some of the intrusions of government, some of the problems of high taxes. Of course, he had learned that in the movies also because when he was a movie actor, the marginal tax rates at that time were over 90 percent."   EDWIN MEESE III

Ronald and Nancy Reagan at their home in Pacific Palisades, California, 1958

Ronald Reagan, Nancy Reagan, Ursula Taylor, Patti Davis, Robert Taylor, and H. Warren Allen at Ron Reagan's christening in California, 1958

Ronald and Nancy Reagan at the victory celebration for the California Governor's race at the Biltmore Hotel in Los Angeles, California, November 8, 1966

In 1966, Ronald Reagan ran for Governor of California and defeated incumbent Democrat Pat Brown by nearly one million votes.

Ronald Reagan being sworn in as Governor of California, Sacramento, California, January 2, 1967

"Ronald Reagan wasn't just an ordinary Republican politician who had drifted into the Republican Party, moved up the ladder, had some skills, got a Republican presidential nomination, and became President. Reagan got into politics because of what he believed." WILLIAM KRISTOL

Ronald Reagan and President Gerald Ford, Republican National Convention, Kansas City, Missouri, August 19, 1976

On August 19, 1976, Reagan's bid for the Republican nomination went all the way to the convention in Kansas City, Missouri, where he lost by a narrow margin to incumbent President Gerald Ford on the first ballot.

Ronald Reagan with his horse Little Man at Rancho del Cielo,
February 1977

Reagan's optimism about America would sustain him. He spent a good
portion of the next four years at his beloved ranch, Rancho del Cielo —
the Ranch in the Sky — just north of Santa Barbara, California.

First Presidential Term
1981-1985

Ronald Reagan campaigns with Nancy Reagan in Columbia, South Carolina, October 10, 1980

In November 1979, Reagan was ready to take one last run for the presidency. He promised to revive the economy, restore the American spirit, and defeat the Soviet Union.

"For our country's future, I pledge you my every effort, I ask for your prayers and your support. I believe that together we can keep this rendezvous with destiny." RONALD REAGAN

President Reagan gives his inaugural address from the U.S. Capitol, Washington, DC, January 20, 1981

In January 1981, Ronald Reagan was sworn in as the 40th President of the United States.

"President Reagan had a reassuring quality, and he had a plan, and most of all, he believed in the American people and their ability to pull themselves through these kinds of problems."

MARLIN FITZWATER

President Ronald Reagan and his Cabinet, February 4, 1981

President Reagan aboard Air Force One

Despite Ronald Reagan's great gift of communication and his ability to connect with the American people, Reagan was described by many as an enigma. His critics mistook his affability for weakness. But behind the smile and the charm existed an extraordinary leader with unique skills and revolutionary ideas.

"The Troika," from left to right: Chief of Staff James Baker III, Counselor to the President Ed Meese, and Deputy Chief of Staff Michael Deaver, at the White House

President Reagan waves to the crowd immediately before being shot in an assassination attempt at the Washington Hilton, March 30, 1981

Chaos outside the Washington Hilton after the assassination attempt on President Reagan. James Brady and police officer Thomas Delahanty lie wounded on the ground, March 30, 1981

President Reagan with Nancy Reagan inside George Washington Hospital four days after the shooting, April 3, 1981

President Reagan returned to the White House twelve days after being shot with a new sense of urgency. He wrote in his diary, "From now on I'm going to dedicate my life to God."

President Reagan works on a speech to Congress in the Oval Office, April 28, 1981

President Reagan addresses Congress and the nation on economic recovery, April 28, 1981

Two weeks after returning to the White House, President Reagan received a hero's welcome from Congress.

President Reagan addresses the nation from the Oval Office on tax reduction legislation, July 27, 1981

"People forget that we had a House of Representatives that was dominated by the other party, and we were able to cobble together a majority that permitted us to bring the top marginal tax rate down from 70 percent to 50 percent in 1981." JAMES A. BAKER III

President Reagan meets with the press after signing the Economic Recovery Tax Act of 1981, Rancho del Cielo, Santa Barbara, California, August 13, 1981

President Reagan at Rancho del Cielo, Santa Barbara, California, August 13, 1981

President Reagan and James Baker in the Oval Office, October 28, 1981

America's economic recovery would not come easily. Just a year into his presidency, Reagan faced a recession — the worst economic slowdown since the Great Depression.

"I never will forget it. The President's approval rating went down to 38 percent, and the White House was a bleak and a tad dreary place at that time. And I know the President was concerned about it, but he was never totally dispirited, he never gave up." JAMES A. BAKER III

President Reagan works at his desk in the Oval Office, May 6, 1982

President and Nancy Reagan at Edwards Air Force Base, July 4, 1982

President Reagan shakes hands with a visitor to the White House, August 17, 1982

President Reagan "punches" Muhammad Ali in the Oval Office, January 24, 1983

Nancy Reagan surprises President Reagan with a birthday cake, February 4, 1983

President Reagan signs the Social Security Amendments Act of 1983 on the South Lawn, April 20, 1983

In 1983, after sixteen months of a recession, Americans went back to work. President Reagan's tax cuts, combined with deregulation, created seven years of unprecedented economic growth.

President Reagan visits Bethesda, Maryland, June 5, 1983

"He understood what made American capitalism work. He understood that the free market is far better than government bureaucracy in controlling the economy." LINDA CHAVEZ

President Reagan and Congressman Newt Gingrich meet in the Cabinet Room, June 24, 1983

President Reagan and Congressman Newt Gingrich on Air Force One, August 1, 1983

President Reagan works in the Cabinet Room, December 5, 1983

While the economy recovered, President Reagan turned in earnest toward challenging the Soviets.

Soviet Soldiers march in Red Square, Moscow

In the years leading up to the Reagan presidency, the Soviet Union seemed permanent and unchallengeable.

A Solidarity banner at the Lenin Shipyard, Gdansk, Poland

In September 1980, Solidarity, the first independent trade union in a Soviet-controlled country, was born at the Lenin Shipyard in Gdansk, Poland.

Solidarity Leader, Lech Walesa, at the Lenin Shipyard strikes, August 21, 1980

A year of strikes and protests followed. In December 1981, the regime struck back, declaring martial law and arresting thousands of Solidarity workers, including its leader, Lech Walesa.

President and Nancy Reagan meet Pope John Paul II at the Vatican, June 7, 1982

"Now, we don't know exactly what was said in that meeting. But when the Pope came out, he said Reagan is a man of peace. He genuinely wants disarmament. And that was very significant because what it meant was, the Catholic Church recognized that the President of the United States was inspired and motivated by fundamentally moral and decent sentiments."

JOHN O'SULLIVAN

President Reagan and Prime Minister Thatcher, London, June 9, 1982

In Eastern Europe, Reagan saw an opportunity to support anti-Communist movements. He found allies in Pope John Paul II and British Prime Minister Margaret Thatcher.

The Reagans honor victims of the U.S. Embassy bombing in Beirut, Andrews Air Force Base, April 23, 1983

"I think one of the most important aspects of Reagan's presidency was how much he thoroughly hated war and how reluctant he was to put American troops in harm's way."   LOU CANNON

President Reagan visits the Vietnam Veterans Memorial Wall in Washington, DC, May 1, 1983

The Reagans attend a memorial service at Camp Lejeune, North Carolina, November 4, 1983

"People do not make wars, governments do, and no mother would ever willingly sacrifice her sons for territorial gain, for economic advantage, for ideology. A people free to choose will always choose peace." RONALD REAGAN

President Reagan looks across the DMZ at Guard Post Collier, South Korea, November 13, 1983

"President Reagan always had a dream that many people didn't realize and that was for a nuclear free world. He once told me, he said, 'I don't want to freeze them, I want to get rid of them.'"

MARLIN FITZWATER

President Reagan meets with Pope John Paul II in Fairbanks, Alaska, May 2, 1984

"We're not naïve — we view the current situation in Poland in the gravest of terms, particularly the increasing use of force against an unarmed population, and violations of the basic civil rights of the Polish people." RONALD REAGAN

President and Nancy Reagan walking through the American Cemetery, Normandy, France, June 6, 1984

In June of 1984, to commemorate the 40th anniversary of the D-Day landings in Normandy, President Reagan paid tribute to the Allied Forces and the U.S. Army Rangers who scaled the cliffs at Pointe du Hoc to reclaim the continent for liberty.

Second Presidential Term
1985-1989

President Reagan gives his acceptance speech at the Republican National Convention, Dallas, Texas, August 23, 1984

In 1984, Reagan hit the campaign trail for the last time, determined to continue his policies for a second term as President of the United States.

The Reagans on the campaign trail in Fountain Valley, California, September 3, 1984

President Reagan waves from a limousine in Fairfield, Connecticut, October 26, 1984

President Reagan salutes at a 1984 campaign rally in Media, Pennsylvania, October 29, 1984

"I think that the people of this country agree with us when we say, you ain't seen nothing yet."

RONALD REAGAN

President Reagan is sworn in for a second term at the United States Capitol, January 21, 1985

The President, no longer underestimated by the American public, was re-elected by the largest electoral vote in U.S. history.

President Reagan writes the State of the Union
Address at Camp David, February 2, 1985

President Reagan walks his dog Lucky with Prime Minister Margaret Thatcher in the White House Rose Garden, February 20, 1985

Ronald Reagan adored Margaret Thatcher. She was a Tory and shared his conservative philosophy of keeping intense pressure on the Soviet Union and winning the Cold War.

President and Nancy Reagan celebrate their 33rd wedding anniversary in the Oval Office, March 4, 1985

President Reagan and Nancy Reagan walk their dog Lucky at Camp David, May 18, 1985

President Reagan and Congressman Newt Gingrich in the Oval Office, May 20, 1985

President Reagan in the Oval Office, May 20, 1985

President Reagan at the U.S. Naval Academy, May 22, 1985

President Reagan walks with his Chief of Staff Donald Regan at the White House, July 10, 1985

President Reagan in the Roosevelt Room, September 26, 1985

In his second term, President Reagan returned his focus to challenging the Soviet Union.

President Reagan lays a wreath at the Tomb of the Unknown Soldier, November 11, 1985

"Freedom is never more than one generation away from extinction."   RONALD REAGAN

President Reagan and Soviet General Secretary Gorbachev at Fleur D'Eau, Geneva, Switzerland, November 19, 1985

After Mikhail Gorbachev came to power in 1985, President Reagan proposed a meeting. Reagan's forceful diplomacy would eventually lead to the most important geopolitical changes in modern times.

President Reagan's first meeting with Soviet General Secretary Gorbachev at Fleur D'Eau during the
Geneva Summit in Switzerland, November 19, 1985

President Reagan would later say he agreed with his friend Margaret Thatcher. There was
something "likeable about Gorbachev." Though Reagan quickly saw him in human terms, the
President was blunt about his differences with the Soviet leader.

President Reagan meets with Soviet General Secretary Gorbachev at Maison de Saussure during the Geneva Summit in Switzerland, November 20, 1985

"He saw a vision that no one else had seen. But he also had a strategy to get there. It wasn't just simply increasing the arms race to bankrupt the Soviet system. It was also signaling his commitment to mutual cooperation and a safe passage for the Soviet system out of totalitarianism." KIRON SKINNER

President Reagan at a meeting with Soviet General Secretary Gorbachev at the Soviet Mission during the Geneva Summit, Switzerland, November 20, 1985

Despite his success in Geneva, criticism of Reagan now came from both the left and the right. But Reagan pushed forward toward his next summit with Gorbachev in Reykjavik, Iceland, in October of 1986.

Nancy Reagan and President Reagan say goodbye before his trip to the Reykjavik Summit with General Secretary Mikhail Gorbachev in Iceland, October 9, 1986

President Reagan meets with Soviet General Secretary Gorbachev at Hofdi House during the Reykjavik Summit in Iceland, October 11, 1986

President Reagan and Soviet General Secretary Gorbachev at Hofdi House
during the Reykjavik Summit, Iceland, October 12, 1986

After an overnight session, President Reagan and Secretary Gorbachev
agreed in principle to historic reductions in their nuclear arsenals.

President Reagan and Soviet General Secretary Gorbachev after the last meeting at Hofdi House, Reykjavik, Iceland, October 12, 1986

The summit was perceived to be a failure.

"As it turned out, that next morning Gorbachev said, 'I can live with all those cuts…but you have to tie it all to killing SDI.'" KEN ADELMAN

President Reagan talks on the telephone, April 1, 1987

After Reykjavik, President Reagan kept pressure on the Soviets. He sent Secretary of State George Schultz to Moscow for further arms talks.

President Reagan and Chancellor Helmut Kohl view the Berlin Wall, June 12, 1987

During a tour of Europe in June 1987, President Reagan continued to confront the Soviet dictatorship.

President Reagan gives a speech at the Brandenburg Gate, June 12, 1987

Reagan challenged Gorbachev with perhaps the most famous words of his presidency.

"Mr. Gorbachev, tear down this wall."   RONALD REAGAN

President Reagan at the Brandenburg Gate, June 12, 1987

"There were several of us on the staff who thought maybe that wasn't a good line to leave in there. President Reagan said, 'That doesn't matter, I want to say it and I'm going to say it.'"

MARLIN FITZWATER

President Reagan greets Pope John Paul II at the Miami Airport, September 10, 1987

President Reagan meeting with Pope John Paul II at the Vizcaya Museum in Miami, Florida, September 10, 1987

President Reagan and Soviet General Secretary Gorbachev at the White House, December 8, 1987

That winter Secretary Gorbachev signed a treaty accepting all of President Reagan's previous terms, with no restrictions on the Strategic Defense Initiative (SDI). The President had followed his own path and achieved results his critics never thought possible.

President Reagan and Soviet General Secretary Gorbachev after signing the Intermediate-Range Nuclear Forces Treaty at the White House, December 8, 1987

"For the first time in history, the language of arms control was replaced by arms reduction. In this case the complete elimination of an entire class of U.S. and Soviet nuclear missiles." RONALD REAGAN

President Reagan and Soviet General Secretary Gorbachev in the Oval Office during the Washington Summit, December 9, 1987

"He forced the arms race and spoke about it openly. This actually forced the arms race onto the Soviets and ended up in their collapse. In that sense, he actually played the biggest role in our way to freedom." LECH WALESA

President Reagan and Mikhail Gorbachev at the signing ceremony for the INF Treaty ratification during the Moscow Summit, June 1, 1988

When President Reagan and General Secretary Gorbachev next met in Moscow in May of 1988, the world was rapidly changing. The Soviet Union was withdrawing from Afghanistan, and Lech Walesa would soon be elected President of Poland.

Vaclav Havel, 1989

In Czechoslovakia, the Velvet Revolution swept the Communists out of power and Vaclav Havel into the presidency.

President Reagan and Prime Minister Thatcher in the White House, November 16, 1988

President Reagan acknowledged Prime Minister Margaret Thatcher for her help in confronting the Soviets.

President Reagan and Prime Minister Thatcher review troops on the South Lawn, November 16, 1988

"Thank you, Mr. President, thank you for the summit, thank you for your presidency, thank you for your testament of belief, and God bless America." MARGARET THATCHER

Soviet General Secretary Gorbachev, President Reagan, and Vice President Bush meet in New York, December 7, 1988

As President Reagan had hoped, freedom and democracy were spreading throughout Eastern Europe.

President Reagan talks on the telephone on his last day in the Oval Office, January 20, 1989

Reagan's Revolution had three primary goals: to revive the economy, to restore the American spirit, and to defeat the Soviet Union. As he prepared to leave office, most Americans felt President Reagan had met these promises.

On President Reagan's last day, he salutes as he boards the helicopter at the U.S. Capitol, January 20, 1989

"My fellow Americans, it's been the honor of my life to be your President. So many of you have written the past few weeks to say thanks, but I could say as much to you. As long as we remember our first principles and believe in ourselves, the future will always be ours. And something else we learned: Once you begin a great movement, there's no telling where it ll end. We meant to change a nation, and instead, we changed a world." RONALD REAGAN

Farewell

President Reagan waves goodbye as he departs Washington, DC, January 20, 1989

President Reagan was almost seventy-eight years old when he left the White House in January of 1989. He kept active in his post presidency, writing his memoirs, overseeing the creation of his presidential library, working on the ranch, and meeting with world leaders.

President Reagan returns from riding his horse at Rancho del Cielo, Santa Barbara, California

Reagan loved working the ranch well into his eighties. But family and friends were noticing the former President's memory loss and difficulty with routine tasks.

President Reagan feeds his horse El Alamein at Rancho del Cielo, Santa Barbara, California

President and Nancy Reagan overlooking Lake Lucky at Rancho del Cielo, Santa Barbara, California

In November of 1994, President Reagan faced his future with an honesty and forthrightness most had come to expect. In a letter to the American people, President Reagan announced that he was suffering from Alzheimer's disease.

President Reagan outside the Oval Office

He wrote, "I now begin the journey that will lead me into the sunset of my life. I know that for America there will always be a bright dawn ahead. Thank you, my friends. May God always bless you. Sincerely, Ronald Reagan."

President Ronald Reagan lies in state, June 9, 2004

On June 5, 2004, President Ronald Reagan passed away. A tremendous outpouring of respect and gratitude followed.

President Ronald Reagan at the White House

President Ronald Reagan, the citizen politician, changed America and the world.

The Filming of
RONALD REAGAN
Rendezvous with Destiny

Executive Producers and Hosts, Newt Gingrich and Callista Gingrich, film *Ronald Reagan: Rendezvous with Destiny* at the Reagan Presidential Library, Simi Valley, California, May 22, 2008

Newt Gingrich and Producer, David Bossie, at the Reagan Presidential Library, Simi Valley, California, May 22, 2008

Newt Gingrich reflects upon President Reagan while filming at the Reagan Presidential Library, Simi Valley, California, May 22, 2008

Callista Gingrich and Writer and Director, Kevin Knoblock, review footage at the Reagan Presidential Library, Simi Valley, California, May 22, 2008

Newt Gingrich and Callista Gingrich film *Ronald Reagan: Rendezvous with Destiny* at the Reagan Presidential Library, Simi Valley, California, May 22, 2008

Newt Gingrich and Callista Gingrich film at Rancho del Cielo, Santa Barbara, California, May 22, 2008

Rancho del Cielo, Santa Barbara, California, May 22, 2008

Callista Gingrich and Kevin Knoblock review footage at Rancho del Cielo, Santa Barbara, California, May 22, 2008

Newt Gingrich, Kevin Knoblock, and Callista Gingrich at Rancho del Cielo, Santa Barbara, California, May 22, 2008

Newt Gingrich, Callista Gingrich, and U.S. Secret Service Agent, John Barletta, at Rancho del Cielo, Santa Barbara, California, May 22, 2008

Newt Gingrich stands by the table where President Reagan signed his tax cuts into law at Rancho del Cielo, Santa Barbara, California, May 22, 2008

President Reagan's boots at Rancho del Cielo, Santa Barbara, California, May 22, 2008

The Reagans' pillow at Rancho del Cielo, Santa Barbara, California, May 22, 2008

David Bossie, Callista Gingrich, Newt Gingrich, and Kevin Knoblock, review the movie script for *Ronald Reagan: Rendezvous with Destiny* at Rancho del Cielo, Santa Barbara, California, May 22, 2008

The living room at Rancho del Cielo, Santa Barbara, California, May 22, 2008

"Most people expected some big mansion, and they're all shocked how modest the ranch is, and how comfortable Ronald Reagan felt." JOHN BARLETTA

Associate Producer, Vince Haley, and Researcher, Rick Tyler, at Rancho del Cielo, Santa Barbara, California, May 22, 2008

Cast and Crew of *Ronald Reagan: Rendezvous with Destiny* at Rancho del Cielo, Santa Barbara, California, May 22, 2008

American Cemetery, Normandy, France, June 23, 2008

Omaha Beach, Normandy, France, June 23, 2008

Newt Gingrich and Callista Gingrich at Pointe du Hoc, Normandy, France, June 23, 2008

Pointe du Hoc, Normandy, France, June 23, 2008

Newt Gingrich and Kevin Knoblock at Pointe du Hoc, Normandy, France, June 23, 2008

Filming at Pointe du Hoc, Normandy, France, June 23, 2008

David Bossie and Newt Gingrich at Pointe du Hoc, Normandy, France, June 23, 2008

Cast and crew of *Ronald Reagan: Rendezvous with Destiny* at Pointe du Hoc, June 23, 2008

Newt Gingrich and Callista Gingrich film at the Lenin Shipyard, Gdansk, Poland, June 24, 2008

Solidarity Monument, Lenin Shipyard, Gdansk, Poland, June 24, 2008

Newt and Callista Gingrich interview President Lech Walesa, Gdansk, Poland, June 24, 2008

Newt Gingrich and Callista Gingrich with President Lech Walesa, Gdansk, Poland, June 24, 2008

Newt Gingrich films at the Lenin Shipyard, Gdansk, Poland, June 24, 2008

Newt Gingrich at the Lenin Shipyard, Gdansk, Poland, June 24, 2008

David Bossie, President of Citizens United, and his wife, Susan Bossie, with President Vaclav Havel, Prague, Czech Republic, June 25, 2008

Cast and crew of *Ronald Reagan: Rendezvous with Destiny* with President Vaclav Havel, Prague, Czech Republic, June 25, 2008

Acknowledgements
by Newt and Callista Gingrich

Thank you to the remarkable group of dedicated people who made this book possible.

We would like to thank our Producer, David Bossie, our Writer and Director, Kevin Knoblock, and the entire team at Citizens United Productions.

Special thanks to our Photographic Editor, Dain Valverde, Director of Photography, Matthew Taylor, and Production Coordinator, Lauren Fleming. Their assistance in this project has been invaluable.

Our deepest gratitude goes to our Editor, Michelle Selesky, who has been tremendously helpful in putting this photographic essay together. Thanks, as well, to Kathy Lubbers, the President of Gingrich Communications, who has been instrumental in orchestrating this project.

We are grateful to David Dunham, Emily Prather, and Mary Sue Englund, for their creative contributions. Dunham Books has been remarkable in turning this book into a reality.

Thanks to American Enterprise Institute Scholars, Steve Hayward and Leon Aron, whose research on the Reagan presidency and the end of the Soviet Union has been most insightful.

Finally, we want to acknowledge our grandchildren, Maggie and Robert Cushman. It is our hope that they will always enjoy the legacy of freedom left for us by President Ronald Reagan.

Acknowledgements
by David N. Bossie

Thank you to my dear friends Newt and Callista Gingrich for their time and dedication to this entire project. Without them, *"Ronald Reagan: Rendezvous with Destiny"* could not have been made.

I would like to thank Writer and Director, Kevin Knoblock, Director of Photography and Editor, Matthew Taylor, Photographic Editor, Dain Valverde, as well as Michael Boos, Lauren Catts, JT Mastranadi, and the rest of the Citizens United Productions team for making the film on which this book is based come to life.

Special gratitude to Lauren Fleming and Jennifer Harris for helping produce the film, as well as leading our European travel.

Lastly, my wife Susan and my children Isabella, Griffin, Lily Campbell, and Maggie Reagan. Their futures are brighter because of Ronald Reagan's presidency.

Photographic Credits